INFUSED

—Water and Ice—

PUMP UP YOUR AGUA WITH
OVER 100 RECIPES!

13-Digit ISBN: 978-1604337938
10-Digit ISBN: 1604337931

This book may be ordered by mail from the publisher. Please include $5.99 for postage and handling.
Please support your local bookseller first!

Books published by Cider Mill Press Book Publishers are available at special discounts for bulk purchases in the United States by corporations, institutions, and other organizations. For more information, please contact the publisher.

Cider Mill Press Book Publishers
"Where Good Books Are Ready for Press"
PO Box 454
12 Spring Street
Kennebunkport, Maine 04046
Visit us online! www.cidermillpress.com

Typography: Bushcraft, Fenwick Park JF, Helvetica Rounded, Neutraface 2 Text, Sentinel
Photography paired with recipes, as well as some supplemental art, by Amy Hunter; all other images used under official license from Shutterstock.com

Printed in China
1 2 3 4 5 6 7 8 9 0
First Edition

INFUSED

—Water and Ice—

PUMP UP YOUR AGUA WITH OVER 100 RECIPES!

AMY HUNTER

CIDER MILL PRESS

BOOK PUBLISHERS

KENNEBUNKPORT, MAINE

Contents

Introduction

Years ago, I drank diet soda like it was going out of style. I worked long hours on my feet and the caffeine and artificial sugar kept me going like nothing else could.

Quitting was hard. Mostly because I was addicted, but also because no matter how many times someone told me to drink more water, I couldn't believe that soda was that much worse. After all, soda is mostly water, right?

Eventually, I managed to quit, and I'm proud to say I haven't had a soda in years. I've reaped plenty of benefits since quitting: My skin is clearer, I'm much less tired, and I've saved tons of money by skipping pricey 12 packs.

While I have no desire to go back to drinking soda, getting enough water is still hard. It's bland, tasteless, and not as refreshing as a fizzy soda. Water's so boring, it can be hard to enjoy it.

This is why we buy high-tech water bottles that connect to your phone and remind you to keep chugging. It's why there's a whole aisle in the supermarket full of no-calorie, flavored waters and additives you can use to make your water more palatable.

These things help, and it's hard to argue against anything that helps you hydrate. But what if you want your water to taste good without relying on sketchy artificial flavorings or mysterious packets of powder that say they don't contain sugar, but don't say what they *do* contain?

There is a way to drink more water, enjoy it, and even get a few nutrients along the way.

It's called infusion, and while that may sound a bit fancy, it's actually very simple. In fact, if you've ever had water with a slice of lemon in it, you've had infused water.

Lemon is just the start, as you will see in this book. Infusing water is easy, delicious, and even kind of fun.

So if you're tired of forcing yourself to drink plain, boring water, keep reading to see what you need to get going.

Before You Start

Infusing your water is easy, but there are some things that will make it easier, and that's what this section is for. Here you'll learn everything you need to know about infusion. You'll see which ingredients are best, and see just how drinking infused water can benefit your health.

BASICS OF INFUSION

Infusion is pretty simple. When you infuse your water with fruit, vegetables, or herbs, you're essentially taking the oils and aromas from the plants and adding them to your water. The result is water that tastes amazing. It won't taste artificial like the flavored bottled water available at the store. It'll taste like the actual ingredients you're using.

The longer you leave your ingredients in the water, the more flavor and aroma you'll get.

Why Infuse?

There are numerous reasons why you want to infuse water. Besides the obvious fact that it just tastes better, you're getting nutrients from the fruits, vegetables, and other ingredients. This can make you feel a little bit better about not always getting the recommended amount of fruits and vegetables.

And let's not forget what drinking enough water will do for you. Here are just a few of the benefits you'll reap by upping your daily intake:

- More energy
- Less fatigue
- Clearer skin
- Improved digestion
- Fewer muscle cramps and sprains
- Fewer headaches

Once you add fruits, you're getting antioxidants, vitamins, and minerals you wouldn't get otherwise. As you can see, infusing water is a great step toward better health and wellness.

INGREDIENTS

You only need a few ingredients to infuse water, but the quality of those ingredients is important.

Water

Clean, fresh-tasting water is imperative for making healthy, delicious infused water. If the water from your tap is suitable for drinking, you can probably use it, but even the best tap water benefits from the use of a filter. You can also use bottled water if that's what you typically drink in your household.

Sparkling Vs. Still

While still water is easiest for infusing water, you can also use sparkling for an experience that is a little more soda-like. There are three types of sparkling water: seltzer, club soda, and sparkling mineral water.

If you want to go the sparkling route, seltzer is the best choice for the recipes in this book — it's got a much cleaner, neutral taste, is easy to find, and is inexpensive. Club soda can also be used, but it will have a stronger taste due to minerals added during processing. Sparkling mineral

water can have a very heavy taste, and the flavors of the minerals may compete with the ingredients used to infuse your water. It is not recommended for the recipes in this book.

Remember when using sparkling water that it will go flat if not properly sealed. If you're going to make a sparkling infusion, make sure you drink it as soon as possible.

Fruits and Vegetables

Almost any fruit or vegetable can be used to infuse water. Some produce is more suitable, such as citrus or cucumbers, but with a bit of effort, you can infuse almost anything.

You want to start with the freshest produce possible. Frozen, dried, or freeze-dried fruits and vegetables do not work well for infusing your water, so stick to fresh. While you may not regularly buy organic produce, you should at least consider it for your infusions, since soaking the fruits and vegetables will release their oils and essences into the water.

Whether organic or conventional, you should thoroughly wash any produce you're going to infuse, even if you think it's already been washed.

Herbs

Herbs are an excellent way to infuse your water with flavor. Soft, leafy herbs like basil and mint add a lot of flavor in a short amount of time. Herbs that have tough stems—like thyme or rosemary—may need more time to infuse, but crushing them helps. Most herbs are fairly easy to grow, which will cut down on costs and ensure that they are grown without harmful chemicals and pesticides that will leach into your water.

Flowers

Flowers can add delicate flavors to your water, and pair nicely with fresh fruits. But you'll want to take a few precautions before adding them to your infusions.

First, you want to make sure you are using edible flower varieties. This is an important distinction because non-edible flowers can be poisonous. While roses are perfectly edible, daffodils are toxic and can make you sick. If you are ever unsure whether a flower is edible, it's a good idea to find something else.

Next, like any other plant you want to add to your water, you should make sure the flowers you use are grown without pesticides or chemicals. If you can grow them yourself, that's always the best option. Unlike fruits, dried flower petals will work fine for your infusions.

Extracts and Essential Oils

Besides extracting the oils and flavors from whole fruits, vegetables, or other plants, there are two other ways to add flavor to your water: Extracts and essential oils.

If you've ever baked, you probably used an extract. Vanilla extract is a common ingredient in cakes, cookies, and even whipped cream.

While you may have used it, you may not understand what it is, so I'll give you a quick rundown. Extracts are essentially an infusion in themselves, with the flavor infused in alcohol. The key ingredients in your extract — vanilla beans, almonds, lemon peel — are simply infused in an alcohol, such as vodka or bourbon. There are alcohol-free extracts, but they can be expensive or difficult to find.

Essential oils, on the other hand, are much more potent than extracts. Essential oils are the oils of the plant itself and are not diluted the way extracts are. They are used most often in aromatherapy, but some can be added to food for additional flavor. They are extremely concentrated, so if you're thinking about adding essential oils to your water, start with a drop at a time.

While these oils may seem like an easy way to add a lot of flavor to your water without the hassle of chopping or muddling fresh fruit, it's important to take precautions when using essential oils. First, not all oils are safe for internal use. Just because it comes from a plant does not mean it's okay to consume.

Next, remember that oil and water don't mix, so when you add a drop of essential oil to your water, it sits on the top. One gulp and all that flavor is gone, and that sip probably won't be very appealing. The only way to get the flavor into your water is to add it to something else first, such as honey.

The recipes in this book rely on whole plants for infusing water. It takes a bit longer, but the results are consistent, safe, and inexpensive. There are a few recipes that use extracts or oils, but I always try to use fresh products before resorting to anything else.

Equipment

You need very little equipment to start infusing your own water or making infused ice cubes. In fact, you probably already have everything you need.

For infusing your water, all you need is something to contain your water. A pretty pitcher or large mason jars are perfectly sufficient. If you have a large beverage dispenser that you use for ice tea or even plain water, that will also work. There are plenty of pitchers and water bottles that have strainers and filters, but they can be expensive and unnecessary if you aren't sure whether this is something you will do on a regular basis.

Remember, though, that the larger your container, the more fruit you'll need to infuse. If you've never infused water before, and want to experiment with flavor combinations, a standard quart-sized mason jar is a great way to start.

You'll need a sharp knife for slicing and dicing, and a zester or grater is handy for removing the zest of citrus fruits without getting the bitterness of the pith. For waters that have tiny pieces, a strainer is helpful. One tool you may not have is a muddler, which is used to release the oils and flavors in fresh ingredients. If you have a mortar and pestle, this will work fine. If you don't have either, you can use the handle of a wooden rolling pin, or even just your fingers for soft herbs.

For ice, you'll need ice cube trays with molds in whatever shape you desire.

That's it!

FAQs

How Much Time Do I Need?

The amount of time you need to infuse your water with flavor depends on what you're using to infuse. Adding lemon to your water will flavor it almost instantly. But if you add a harder fruit, a tough herb, or a dried spice, it will take longer.

A good rule of thumb is to let the flavors meld overnight in the fridge, and then strain the ingredients out of the water. Once the ingredients are removed, the water should be safe to drink for several days.

How Long Will My Water Last?

Your infused water should last at least several days if refrigerated, and longer if the water is strained. If you notice any of your ingredients getting moldy, or your water tastes off, it's best to pour it out and start over.

You can also re-infuse the water with the fruit you used. I like to get my water started the night before I'm going to drink it. By the morning, it's pretty fruity and strong. When I'm about halfway through the pitcher, I just add more water and continue to drink. The infusion does get a little bit weaker the more water you add, but it's still delicious, and you're getting the most out of your fruit.

Why Does My Water Taste Bitter?

Citrus fruits like lemons or limes are among the best and easiest fruits to infuse, but if they hang around too long, they will cause your water to taste bitter. You can alleviate this problem by peeling citrus fruits, or removing them after a few hours.

Can I Eat the Fruit That Has Infused My Water?

As long as the fruit is not rotten and doesn't contain mold, you certainly can eat it (although if your fruit is bad, you shouldn't drink the water it's in!).

However, it probably won't taste very good, since all of the flavor and essence should be in your water. Softer fruits, like berries, may also become mushy, particularly if you've muddled them beforehand.

If you simply can't stand the thought of throwing the fruit out, your best bet is to use it in smoothies or other applications. This way, you can still get the fiber and leftover nutrients, and use other ingredients to make it taste good.

Now that you know the basics of infusion, let's move on to the recipes.

Water Recipes

Here you'll find a variety of infused waters to hydrate and delight you. While they will all include some kind of fruit, some of the recipes have other ingredients that play a big part in the flavor and aroma of the finished result. Because of this, the recipes are divided in such a way that you know which flavors will stand out.

Unless specified, the water recipes are all made in 64-ounce quantities, giving you eight servings, enough to drink in a day or two. You can make these in a half-gallon mason jar or in a pitcher. You can also easily make a half-batch if you'd like.

These recipes are easy to prepare and easy to experiment with, so don't feel like you have to stick to the ingredients for each recipe. The only thing you really want to keep in mind is that less is more when it comes to ingredients. Too many, and the flavors get lost — it's just wasted fruit! I like two different fruits and maybe one flavoring ingredient (herb, spice, or flower); generally, anything more than three distinct flavors is asking for trouble.

Fruit

These recipes are nothing more than water and fruit. Since they're pretty hard to get wrong, they're a perfect starting point if you've never infused water. You can easily substitute fruit in equal parts, or even swap still water for sparkling. These are great for backyard barbecues and perfect for kids. These are best made with ripe, seasonal fruits.

Citrus Fizz

This easy-to-drink sparkling water will remind you of your favorite citrus soda, but without all the sugar and calories. It's perfect served over ice on a hot summer day.

1 Place the sliced fruit in a half-gallon pitcher or jar.

2 Pour seltzer water over the ingredients and refrigerate for 2-4 hours, or overnight.

3 Serve chilled.

Tip: If you're not going to drink water made with citrus fruit within two days, be sure to remove the rind in order to prevent bitterness.

INGREDIENTS

2 limes, thinly sliced

1 orange, thinly sliced

1 lemon, thinly sliced

64 ounces seltzer water

Strawberry Lemon

This sweet, tart infusion will remind you of your favorite lemonade, and is the perfect summertime refresher. It's best made with sweet, in-season strawberries that are bursting with flavor.

1 Place the strawberries and lemon in a half-gallon pitcher or jar.

2 Cover with water. Let sit for 1-2 hours at room temperature for a quick infusion, or refrigerate for anywhere from 4 hours to overnight.

3 Serve chilled, and drink within 2 days for optimum results.

INGREDIENTS

1 pint ripe strawberries, hulled and sliced

1 lemon, thinly sliced

64 ounces cold-filtered water

Blackberry Lime

Fresh blackberries and limes are the perfect combo, and one you'll make over and over again.

INGREDIENTS

1 pint ripe blackberries, lightly mashed

2 limes, thinly sliced

64 ounces cold-filtered water

1 Place the berries and lime slices in a half-gallon pitcher or jar.

2 Cover with water. Let sit for 1-2 hours at room temperature for a quick infusion, or refrigerate for anywhere from 4 hours to overnight.

3 Serve chilled, and drink within 2 days for best results.

Tip: When using in-season fruit, such as berries, always taste them before adding them to your water. If they are sweet and juicy, they are perfect. Sour, moldy, or astringent berries will make your water taste just like that — which is not good, especially alongside tart fruit like citrus.

Cherry-Lime Spritzer

Sweet cherries and tart limes explode when added to sparkling water. Make sure you taste the cherries before adding them to your water, and be sure to remove all traces of the pits!

INGREDIENTS

1 cup fresh, sweet cherries, pitted and halved

2 limes, thinly sliced

64 ounces seltzer water

1 Place the fruit in a half-gallon pitcher or jar.

2 Pour seltzer water over the ingredients and refrigerate for 2-4 hours, or overnight.

3 Serve chilled.

Nutrition note: Fresh cherries are loaded with antioxidants, due to the dark color of their skin. The juice can also help you sleep, so if you like something refreshing before bed, try this.

Orange-Ginger Spritzer

Oranges add a hefty dose of vitamin C to this delicious water, while fresh ginger adds a hint of spiciness. It tastes like a fresh ginger ale, and can help heal an upset stomach—just like the processed stuff.

INGREDIENTS

1 orange, thinly sliced

1 two-inch piece of ginger, peeled and smashed with a knife

64 ounces seltzer water

1 Place the orange slices and ginger in a half-gallon pitcher or jar.

2 Pour seltzer water over the ingredients and refrigerate for 2-4 hours, or overnight.

3 Serve chilled.

Tip: To easily peel your ginger, use a spoon instead of a vegetable peeler to remove the skin: simply cut off any thick knots, then use the tip of the spoon to scrape the thin skin away.

Strawberry Grapefruit

Bright and sweet, this water is super refreshing. Because grapefruit is naturally bitter, I like to remove the rind before infusing. If you're going to drink it all in a day, however, you can skip that step.

1 Place the fruit in a half-gallon pitcher or jar.

2 Cover with water. Let sit for 1-2 hours at room temperature for a quick infusion, or refrigerate for anywhere from 4 hours to overnight.

3 Serve chilled.

Warning! Fresh grapefruit can interact poorly with some prescription medicines, so if you take multiple prescriptions, you may want to check with your doctor before consuming this water.

INGREDIENTS

1 pint ripe strawberries, hulled and sliced

1 grapefruit, rind and white pith removed

64 ounces cold-filtered water

Orange Mango

Sweet and tangy, this orange infusion will remind you of a tropical vacation. Make sure your mango is ripe so that your water has the floral aroma and flavor mangoes are known for.

INGREDIENTS

1 orange,
thinly sliced

1 mango, peeled, pit
removed, and diced

64 ounces
cold-filtered water

1 Place the fruit in a half-gallon pitcher or jar.

2 Cover with water. Let sit for 1-2 hours at room temperature for a quick infusion, or refrigerate for anywhere from 4 hours to overnight.

3 Serve chilled.

Mixed Berry

This is perfect for summer, when berries are at their best. Use any combination of berries you like or have on hand, but be sure to mash them lightly so that the juices infuse with the water.

INGREDIENTS

2 cups mixed berries of your choice (strawberries, raspberries, blackberries, or blueberries), lightly mashed

64 ounces cold-filtered water

1 Place the berries in a half-gallon pitcher or jar.

2 Cover with water. Let sit for 1-2 hours at room temperature for a quick infusion, or refrigerate for anywhere from 4 hours to overnight.

3 Serve chilled.

Note: While it might be tempting to buy a bag of frozen mixed berries, please don't. Frozen produce doesn't produce nearly as much juice (read: flavor!) as fresh, so you'll need to use far more to get the same berry flavor.

Blueberry Orange

Sweet, juicy blueberries are a delicious infusion choice, especially when paired with oranges! Make sure to mash the blueberries enough to break the skin; otherwise, you won't get much flavor from them.

1 Place the blueberries and orange slices in a half-gallon pitcher or jar.

2 Cover with water. Let sit for 1-2 hours at room temperature for a quick infusion, or refrigerate for anywhere from 4 hours to overnight.

3 Serve chilled.

INGREDIENTS

1 pint fresh blueberries, lightly mashed

1 orange, thinly sliced

64 ounces cold-filtered water

Blackberry Grapefruit

Grapefruit is delicious with any type of berry, but blackberry just may be my favorite. Just make sure they are sweet and juicy enough to counteract the grapefruit's natural bitterness.

INGREDIENTS

1 pint blackberries, lightly mashed

1 grapefruit, rind and white pith removed

64 ounces cold-filtered water

1 Place the blackberries and grapefruit in a half-gallon pitcher or jar.

2 Cover with water. Let sit for 1-2 hours at room temperature for a quick infusion, or refrigerate for anywhere from 4 hours to overnight.

3 Serve chilled.

Tip: Wash fresh berries right before using to prevent mold and make them last longer.

Lemon-Raspberry Spritzer

MAKES 8 SERVINGS

Lemons and raspberries are a classic combination. Not only do they taste delicious together, you can't help but be happy when you see the bright yellow and red in your water.

1 Place the berries and lemon slices in a half-gallon pitcher or jar.

2 Pour seltzer water over the ingredients and refrigerate for 2-4 hours, or overnight.

3 Serve chilled.

Note: Raspberries are especially delicate, and don't last as long as other berries — make sure to double-check for mold before adding them to your pitcher.

INGREDIENTS

1 pint fresh raspberries

1 lemon, thinly sliced

64 ounces seltzer water

Pineapple Coconut

This is one of the few infused water recipes that doesn't use fresh or sparkling water. Instead, it is made with coconut water. Coconut water is readily available in cartons at your local grocery store, and when it's combined with fresh pineapple, it is heaven in a glass.

INGREDIENTS

32 ounces pure coconut water

1 cup pineapple chunks

1 Combine the coconut water and pineapple chunks in a jar.

2 Refrigerate for 2-4 hours, or overnight.

3 Serve chilled.

Cherry Almond

Cherries and almonds are delicious together, but almonds don't infuse water due to being dry. For this reason, almond extract is perfect. If you think you need more almond flavoring, taste the water first, and then adjust.

1 Place the cherries and almond extract in a half-gallon pitcher or jar.

2 Cover with water. Let sit for 1-2 hours at room temperature for a quick infusion, or refrigerate for anywhere from 4 hours to overnight.

3 Serve chilled.

INGREDIENTS

1 cup fresh, sweet cherries, pitted and halved

½ teaspoon pure almond extract

64 ounces cold-filtered water

Strawberry-Watermelon Fizz

Watermelon is the perfect fruit for infusing water. It's perfect in the summer when watermelon is ripe and extra sweet — the juices infuse the water super-fast. Serve this at a holiday cookout, and watch it disappear!

INGREDIENTS

1 pint ripe strawberries, hulled and sliced

1 cup cubed watermelon

64 ounces seltzer water

1 Place the strawberries and watermelon in a half-gallon pitcher or jar.

2 Pour seltzer water over the ingredients and refrigerate for 2-4 hours, or overnight.

3 Serve chilled.

Tropical Spritzer

You can use any combination of tropical fruit in this water, so don't feel limited by what you see here. This one is great with coconut water as well.

1 Place the fruit in a half-gallon pitcher or jar.

2 Pour seltzer water over the ingredients and refrigerate for 2-4 hours, or overnight.

3 Serve chilled.

INGREDIENTS

1 cup pineapple chunks

½ cup mango chunks

½ cup papaya chunks

64 ounces seltzer water

Stone Fruit Blend

Stone fruits are those with pits — think peaches, plums, and cherries. You can use any combination of fruits here; my favorite is peach and apricot.

INGREDIENTS

2 cups stone fruits, chopped and pitted

64 ounces cold-filtered water

1 Place the chopped fruit in a half-gallon pitcher or jar.

2 Cover with water. Let sit for 1-2 hours at room temperature for a quick infusion, or refrigerate for anywhere from 4 hours to overnight.

3 Serve chilled.

Warning! Make sure to remove all traces of pits from your fruits. The pits of some stone fruits contain arsenic, and while it may take large quantities to become toxic, it's probably better to not ingest it at all.

Vegetable

These waters are still fruity, but the vegetable component makes them slightly earthy. While some kids may like them, they will likely be more appreciated by adults with more refined palates. If you're not sure about the idea of vegetable-flavored water, but still want to try, you can always start with fewer vegetables and add more as you start to become more accustomed to the flavor.

Raspberry-Jalapeño Sparkler

MAKES 8 SERVINGS

If you've ever had a jam made with jalapeños and enjoyed it, you will love this water. It's sweet and spicy all at once, and can be quite refreshing.

INGREDIENTS

1-2 fresh jalapeño peppers

1 pint fresh raspberries, mashed slightly

64 ounces seltzer water

1 Remove the stems from the peppers and cut in half lengthwise. Remove the membrane and seeds and muddle lightly to break up the skin and extract some of the juice.

2 Place the berries and peppers in a half-gallon pitcher or jar.

3 Pour seltzer water over the ingredients and refrigerate for 2-4 hours, or overnight.

4 Serve chilled.

Cilantro Jalapeño Lime

This spicy water has a very vegetal taste, but is delicious. The lime brightens it up and pairs well with the heat from the pepper. You want to drink this one on the same day you make it, as it gets spicier the longer it sits.

INGREDIENTS

- 1-2 jalapeño peppers
- 3 sprigs cilantro
- 1 lime, thinly sliced
- 64 ounces cold-filtered water

1 Remove the stems from the peppers and cut in half lengthwise. Remove the membrane and seeds and muddle lightly to break up the skin and extract some of the juice.

2 Place the peppers, cilantro, and lime slices in a half-gallon pitcher or jar.

3 Cover with water. Let sit for 1-2 hours at room temperature for a quick infusion, or refrigerate for anywhere from 4 hours to overnight.

4 Serve chilled, and drink within 1-2 days.

Substitution Suggestion: If you like extra-hot flavors, you can replace the jalapeños in this water with habaneros.

Apple Fennel

The two main ingredients pair well here, and are especially delicious when left to infuse.

INGREDIENTS

½ small fennel bulb, thinly sliced

1 medium apple, cored and thinly sliced

64 ounces cold-filtered water

1 Place the fennel and apple in a half-gallon pitcher or jar.

2 Cover with water. Let sit for 1-2 hours at room temperature for a quick infusion, or refrigerate for anywhere from 4 hours to overnight.

3 Serve chilled.

Cucumber Ginger Lemongrass

MAKES 8 SERVINGS

This is one of my favorites, and once you taste it, you'll see why. It's very refreshing, not fruity at all, and gets a hint of spice from the ginger. If you can't find fresh lemongrass, a lemon will work, though it will have less of the floral flavor you get from the lemongrass. While most of the waters are fine with either still or sparkling, this one is best with still.

1 Cut the lemongrass into 3-4 inch pieces. Bend them without breaking to help release their oils and juices. Add to a jar or pitcher with the cucumber and ginger.

2 Cover with water. Let sit for 1-2 hours at room temperature for a quick infusion, or refrigerate for anywhere from 4 hours to overnight.

3 Serve chilled.

INGREDIENTS

2 stalks fresh lemongrass

½ cucumber, thinly sliced, seeds removed

1 1-inch piece of ginger, peeled and smashed

64 ounces cold-filtered water

Flowers

The recipes in this section all contain, you guessed it — flowers! They are fruity and floral, and have a relaxing quality, kind of like a nice cup of tea. You can serve these waters chilled, but they are delicious at room temperature as well.

I like to make these waters for a baby or bridal shower, Easter brunch, or any occasion where flowers are on display. They're delightful in the spring and add a pinch of charm and calm to any event.

Strawberry Hibiscus

MAKES 8 SERVINGS

Hibiscus flowers are tart like cranberries, and will likely cause your water to turn a bright pink or red. They are delicious with sweet, aromatic, and in-season strawberries.

INGREDIENTS

3-4 fresh or dried hibiscus flowers

1 pint fresh strawberries, hulled and sliced

64 ounces cold-filtered water

1 Place the hibiscus flowers and strawberries in a half-gallon pitcher or jar.

2 Cover with water. Let sit for 1-2 hours at room temperature for a quick infusion, or refrigerate for anywhere from 4 hours to overnight.

3 Serve chilled.

Blueberry Lavender

This water is perfect for a baby shower, brunch, or any other occasion where you want something elegant. You can use fresh or dried lavender, but make sure it's safe for culinary use.

1 Place the lavender and blueberries in a half-gallon pitcher or jar.

2 Cover with water. Let sit for 1-2 hours at room temperature for a quick infusion, or refrigerate for anywhere from 4 hours to overnight.

3 Strain before serving. Can be served chilled or at room temperature.

Warning! Less is definitely more when it comes to lavender, especially dried. You want a nice, subtle background flavor; use too much, and it will make your water taste like soap.

INGREDIENTS

1-2 fresh lavender sprigs, or ½ teaspoon dried

1 cup fresh blueberries, lightly muddled to break the skin

64 ounces cold-filtered water

Lemon Lavender

Lemon and lavender are an intoxicating combination, especially on a stressful day. If you drink water before bedtime, try a glass of this one at room temperature.

INGREDIENTS

1-2 fresh lavender sprigs or ½ teaspoon dried

1 lemon, thinly sliced

64 ounces cold-filtered water

1 Place the lavender and lemon in a half-gallon pitcher or jar.

2 Cover with water. Let sit for 1-2 hours at room temperature for a quick infusion, or refrigerate for anywhere from 4 hours to overnight.

3 Strain before serving. Serve chilled or at room temperature.

Vanilla Lemon Violet

Violets have light notes of vanilla, which makes them wonderful with vanilla bean and lemon. This water is a nice touch for a spring brunch or bridal shower; it's especially lovely in a punch bowl with lemon slices and violets floating on top. You can substitute a teaspoon of pure vanilla extract for the vanilla bean if you'd like.

1 Place the violet petals, lemon slices, and vanilla component in a half-gallon pitcher or jar.

2 Cover with water. Let sit for 1-2 hours at room temperature for a quick infusion, or refrigerate for anywhere from 4 hours to overnight.

3 Serve chilled or at room temperature.

Tip: If you've never used a whole vanilla bean before, don't worry, it's easy: Using a sharp knife, slice down the center of the bean lengthwise (it's okay if you accidentally cut it in half.) Scrape all those tiny black seeds into your water, since that's where the flavor is. Then add the whole bean to your pitcher.

INGREDIENTS

½ cup violet petals

1 lemon, thinly sliced

1 vanilla bean, sliced down the center or 1 teaspoon pure vanilla extract

64 ounces cold-filtered water

Lemon Rosewater

I've made this with both rose petals and rosewater extract, and while both are delicious, I actually prefer the extract, even though rose petals are prettier. You should try both ways to see which one is your favorite.

INGREDIENTS

½ cup rose petals or 1 teaspoon rosewater extract

1 lemon, thinly sliced

64 ounces cold-filtered water

1 Place the lemon slices and rose component in a half-gallon pitcher or jar.

2 Cover with water. Let sit for 1-2 hours at room temperature for a quick infusion, or refrigerate for anywhere from 4 hours to overnight.

3 Serve chilled or at room temperature.

Strawberry Chamomile

Chamomile flowers are light, sweet, and herbal. I've tried them with other fruits, but strawberry is by far their best partner. This water is relaxing, fragrant, and a nice, healthy stress reliever when you want to have a cocktail but know better. It's best at room temperature.

1 Place the chamomile flowers and strawberries in a half-gallon pitcher or jar.

2 Cover with water. Let sit for 1-2 hours at room temperature for a quick infusion, or refrigerate for anywhere from 4 hours to overnight.

3 Serve at room temperature.

INGREDIENTS

¼ cup dried chamomile flowers

1 pint fresh strawberries, hulled and sliced

64 ounces cold-filtered water

Herbs and Spices

Herbs and spices are excellent for infusing water. Fresh herbs infuse nicely and fast, especially when muddled slightly to release some of their oils. Also, herbs are really easy to grow, which means you'll always have a healthy supply on hand.

Whole spices, on the other hand, may need to steep a bit longer in order to infuse your water. But once you taste it, you'll agree that it's worth the effort. Make sure you don't use powdered spices, unless specifically directed — they'll give your water a poor mouth feel that is hard to get rid of, even with straining.

Apple Cinnamon

There's nothing quite like the combination of apple and cinnamon, especially in the fall. This water is perfect for Halloween parties, or any other event you may be having during the late summer or early autumn. This water is super-easy to make, but it takes longer to infuse, so plan accordingly.

1 Place the apple and cinnamon sticks in a half-gallon pitcher or jar.

2 Cover with water. Infuse for at least 4 hours, but up to overnight for maximum flavor.

3 Serve chilled.

INGREDIENTS

1 large apple, cored and thinly sliced

2 cinnamon sticks

64 ounces cold-filtered water

Pear Anise

Anise is a strong, licorice-flavored spice that pairs perfectly with fall fruits like pears. Don't go overboard with it here or it may become overpowering; a few small, cracked pieces are all you need.

INGREDIENTS

2-3 broken pieces of star anise

1 medium ripe pear, cored, stemmed, and thinly sliced

64 ounces cold-filtered water

1 Place the star anise and pear in a half-gallon pitcher or jar.

2 Cover with water. Let sit for 1-2 hours at room temperature for a quick infusion, or refrigerate for anywhere from 4 hours to overnight.

3 Serve chilled.

Orange Chai

There are many variations of chai spice, but this blend is my favorite. This is one of the few water recipes I like that have more than a few ingredients, and that's only because you need all of these spices to get an authentic flavor. Due to the hardness of the spices, a long soaking is good for this one, so I like to peel the rind off my oranges.

1 Place the orange, cardamom pods, cinnamon stick, cloves, bay leaf, peppercorns, and ginger in a half-gallon pitcher or jar.

2 Cover with water. Infuse for at least 4 hours, but up to overnight for maximum flavor.

3 Strain and serve chilled.

INGREDIENTS

1 orange, peeled, white pith removed

2 cardamom pods, cracked

1 cinnamon stick

2 whole cloves

1 bay leaf

3-4 whole black peppercorns

1 1-inch piece of ginger, peeled and smashed

64 ounces cold-filtered water

Apple Chai Spritzer

This is another delicious blend of chai spice! While there are more than a few ingredients, it's worth it for the authentic flavor alone. Due to the hardness of the spices, a long soaking is good for this recipe.

INGREDIENTS

1 large apple, cored and thinly sliced

2 cardamom pods, cracked

1 cinnamon stick

2 whole cloves

1 bay leaf

3-4 whole black peppercorns

1 1-inch piece of ginger, peeled and smashed

64 ounces seltzer water

1 Place the fruit and flavoring ingredients in a half-gallon pitcher or jar.

2 Pour the seltzer water over the ingredients and refrigerate overnight, or longer.

3 Strain and serve chilled.

Strawberry Basil Lemon

MAKES 8 SERVINGS

Strawberries and basil are a perfect summer combination — sweet and fruity, with a fresh bite from the basil. The lemon gives it a mild tartness that pulls it all together.

1 Place the strawberries, lemon, and basil in a half-gallon pitcher or jar.

2 Cover with water. Let sit for 1-2 hours at room temperature for a quick infusion, or refrigerate for anywhere from 4 hours to overnight.

3 Serve chilled.

Tip: Muddling basil and other delicate leaves releases the plant's oils, but don't overdo it. You want to just lightly rub the leaves with your muddler, not break them up.

INGREDIENTS

1 pint fresh strawberries, hulled and sliced

1 lemon, thinly sliced

3-4 basil leaves, lightly muddled

64 ounces cold-filtered water

Vanilla Cinnamon Orange

Vanilla and cinnamon add an intoxicating aroma to the bright flavor of orange in this dreamy water. It will remind you of a Creamsicle, but better!

INGREDIENTS

1 orange, thinly sliced

1 cinnamon stick

1 vanilla bean, sliced lengthwise

64 ounces cold-filtered water

1 Place the orange, cinnamon stick, and vanilla bean in a half-gallon pitcher or jar.

2 Cover with water. Let sit for 1-2 hours at room temperature for a quick infusion, or refrigerate for anywhere from 4 hours to overnight.

3 Serve chilled.

Tip: If you've never used a whole vanilla bean before, don't worry, it's easy: Using a sharp knife, slice down the center of the bean lengthwise (it's okay if you accidentally cut it in half.) Scrape all those tiny black seeds into your water, since that's where the flavor is. Then add the whole bean to your pitcher.

Cinnamon Grape

Grapes are excellent for infusing water. They're juicy and sweet, and flavor the water quickly. The cinnamon here adds a hint of spice that is surprisingly delicious. You can use either red or green grapes here.

1 Place the grapes and cinnamon stick in a half-gallon pitcher or jar.

2 Cover with water. Let sit for 1-2 hours at room temperature for a quick infusion, or refrigerate for anywhere from 4 hours to overnight.

3 Serve chilled.

INGREDIENTS

1 cup grapes, halved and seeded

1 cinnamon stick

64 ounces cold-filtered water

Watermelon Mint Sparkler

If you want something refreshing, this is it. Fresh mint leaves impart an amazing flavor that is difficult to get from any other source. And they are simply outstanding when paired with juicy watermelon.

INGREDIENTS

2 sprigs fresh mint, muddled

1 cup cubed watermelon, seeds removed

64 ounces seltzer water

1 Place the mint and watermelon in a half-gallon pitcher or jar.

2 Pour seltzer water over the ingredients and refrigerate for 2-4 hours, or overnight.

3 Serve chilled.

Kiwi Honeydew Thyme

This infusion is juicy, but with an herbal quality that is surprisingly good. For a slight variation, you can substitute cantaloupe for the honeydew.

1 Place the kiwi, honeydew melon, and thyme in a half-gallon pitcher or jar.

2 Cover with water. Let sit for 1-2 hours at room temperature for a quick infusion, or refrigerate for anywhere from 4 hours to overnight.

3 Strain to remove the thyme, if desired. Serve chilled.

INGREDIENTS

1 kiwi, peeled, sliced, and lightly muddled

1 cup cubed honeydew melon

1 sprig fresh thyme

64 ounces cold-filtered water

Cucumber Mint

Cucumber is often paired with mint in salads and other recipes, so it's no surprise that it's delicious this way. Still, you'll be taken aback by how good this.

INGREDIENTS

2-3 fresh mint sprigs

1 small cucumber, seeded and sliced

64 ounces cold-filtered water

1 Place the mint and cucumber in a half-gallon pitcher or jar.

2 Cover with water. Let sit for 1-2 hours at room temperature for a quick infusion, or refrigerate for anywhere from 4 hours to overnight.

3 Serve chilled.

Cucumber Pear Rosemary

MAKES 8 SERVINGS

It seems like the flavors would compete with each other in this one, but it actually comes together quite nicely. With a hint of sweetness, a revitalizing bite, and herby flavor, it may just become your new favorite.

1 Place the cucumber, pear, and rosemary in a half-gallon pitcher or jar.

2 Cover with water. Let sit for 1-2 hours at room temperature for a quick infusion, or refrigerate for anywhere from 4 hours to overnight.

3 Serve chilled.

INGREDIENTS

1 small cucumber, seeded and sliced

1 medium ripe pear, cored and thinly sliced

1 sprig fresh rosemary

64 ounces cold-filtered water

Chocolate Mint

One of my favorite flavor combinations is chocolate and mint, so naturally this water is one of my all-time favorites. I've tried making it with cacao nibs, but they just don't impart as much chocolate flavor as the extract, so that's what I recommend here.

INGREDIENTS

2-3 sprigs fresh mint

1 teaspoon pure chocolate extract

64 ounces cold-filtered water

1 Place the mint and chocolate extract in a half-gallon pitcher or jar.

2 Cover with water. Let sit for 1-2 hours at room temperature for a quick infusion, or refrigerate for anywhere from 4 hours to overnight.

3 Serve chilled.

Note: If you can find a bunch of chocolate mint, I urge you to try it here. It's exactly what it sounds like: a mint plant that has the aroma of chocolate. It is heavenly. I've found it at my local farmers' market, but not often, so keep an eye out!

Pineapple Mint

This super-sweet, super-refreshing water is one of the most flavorful ones I've ever made, and it doesn't take a long infusion to get there. This one is perfect when you want to whip something up on short notice, but still want full flavor.

1 Place the pineapple and fresh mint in a half-gallon pitcher or jar.

2 Cover with water. Let sit for 1-2 hours at room temperature for a quick infusion, or refrigerate for anywhere from 4 hours to overnight.

3 Serve chilled.

INGREDIENTS

1 cup pineapple chunks

2-3 sprigs fresh mint

64 ounces
cold-filtered water

Lemon Verbena Thyme

This infusion is one of a few that doesn't need fruit to make it good. It's fragrant, herbaceous, and perfect in the summer. If you can't find lemon verbena in your local supermarket, try a farmers' market or specialty store.

INGREDIENTS

1 sprig fresh thyme

2-3 sprigs lemon verbena

64 ounces cold-filtered water

1 Place the thyme and lemon verbena in a half-gallon pitcher or jar.

2 Cover with water. Let sit for 1-2 hours at room temperature for a quick infusion, or refrigerate for anywhere from 4 hours to overnight.

3 Serve chilled.

Citrus Sage Pineapple

One of my favorite nighttime teas, which is made with lavender, sage, and citrus, inspired this recipe. To make it more refreshing, I use fresh pineapple, which pairs beautifully with the distinct warmth of sage.

INGREDIENTS

½ lemon, thinly sliced

½ orange, thinly sliced

1 cup pineapple chunks

4-5 fresh sage leaves

64 ounces cold-filtered water

1 Place the lemon, orange, pineapple, and sage in a half-gallon pitcher or jar.

2 Cover with water. Let sit for 1-2 hours at room temperature for a quick infusion, or refrigerate for anywhere from 4 hours to overnight.

3 Serve chilled.

Lemon Blackberry Mint Spritzer

Lemons and mint are a classic combination for infusing water, but when you add blackberries, they become magical. Sweet, tart, and minty, this drink is refreshing, thirst quenching, and addictive.

INGREDIENTS

1 pint fresh blackberries, lightly mashed

1 lemon, thinly sliced

2-3 sprigs fresh mint

64 ounces seltzer water

1 Place the blackberries, lemon, and mint in a half-gallon pitcher or jar.

2 Pour seltzer water over the ingredients and refrigerate for 2-4 hours, or overnight.

3 Serve chilled.

Citrus Rosemary

This water can be made with any type of citrus you like. I'm partial to a combination of orange and grapefruit, which is what I use here, but experiment with your favorites until you find your preference.

1 Place the orange, grapefruit, and rosemary in a half-gallon pitcher or jar.

2 Cover with water. Let sit for 1-2 hours at room temperature for a quick infusion, or refrigerate for anywhere from 4 hours to overnight.

3 Serve chilled.

INGREDIENTS

1 orange, thinly sliced

½ grapefruit, thinly sliced

1 sprig fresh rosemary

64 ounces cold-filtered water

About Infused Ice

Infused ice is similar to infused water, except in the form of ice cubes. You can infuse ice cubes in a couple of different ways; the best method depends on how you're going to use the ice.

You can make infused ice either by adding pieces of fruit to your ice cube tray and pouring water over them, or by pureeing your ingredients in a blender and pouring that mixture into ice cube trays. I tend to like the first method best; it's easier, and I like the look of fruit pieces in the ice better than just a solid, colored cube.

Besides the flavor infused ice provides, another benefit of making it is the visual effect it provides. What could be prettier than a crystal-clear ice cube with brightly colored pieces of fruit in the middle?

Unfortunately, without some preparation, simply pouring tap water over fruit and freezing it will result in cloudy cubes. You'll still be able to see the fruit, but it's not nearly as pretty if you're serving this at a party where you want your efforts to stand out.

Luckily, it's not that difficult to achieve perfectly clear ice cubes, and it doesn't require any special equipment. Below is the method I use, and it works great every time.

For the clearest cubes, use distilled water. The distilling process removes most of the air and minerals from your water, which are what causes ice to become cloudy. Filtered bottled water is a good second choice.

Before you place the water in the trays, you're going to want to boil it twice. A teakettle is best for this, as it allows for easy pouring into ice cube trays. Fill your teakettle with water, boil, let cool, boil a second time, and let cool again.

Now your water is ready to use. While this process does take a bit longer, the visual results are worth it—if that's what you're going for. Of course, if you're just making ice to add to the water bottle you take to work with you, you can skip this step entirely, as it won't affect the flavor of your ice cubes.

The recipes in this section make 24 standard-sized (1-ounce) ice cubes. You don't have to use ice cube trays — silicone muffin tins, candy molds, even Styrofoam egg cartons can be used to make ice. Just about anything that can hold water can be used, with the exception of glass, which can break from expansion. Just make sure your mold is safe for food, since you will be consuming these!

And always remember, if you don't boil your water twice before making your cubes, they will turn cloudy!

Fruit

These fruit-heavy recipes are great for adding to water, lemonade, or iced tea, since they impart a juicy flavor and aroma. They are also a perfect starting point for making infused ice cubes. So get those knives sharpened and get that teakettle ready—it's time to infuse some life into your ice!

Simple Citrus Cubes

MAKES 24 ICE CUBES

These are perfect for flavoring plain water, so having a big batch on hand means you'll never have to drink unflavored water again. Use any combination of citrus fruit you like.

INGREDIENTS

½ lemon, sliced, seeds removed

½ lime, sliced

½ orange, sliced, seeds removed

24 ounces filtered or distilled water

1 Chop up your fruit so that the pieces will fit in your ice cube tray, and put the pieces in each individual mold.

2 Pour water into the tray, and carefully transfer the tray to the freezer. Freeze until the cubes are solid, and then use in your drink of choice.

Blood Orange Raspberry

These brightly colored cubes are sweet and tart, and delicious in iced tea.

1 Chop up your fruit so the pieces will fit in your ice cube tray, and place the pieces in each individual mold.

2 Pour water into the trays, and carefully transfer the tray to the freezer. Freeze until the cubes are solid, and then use in your drink of choice.

INGREDIENTS

1 pint fresh raspberries, lightly muddled

1 blood orange, sliced, seeds removed

24 ounces filtered or distilled water

Blueberry Lemon

This classic combination makes perfect ice cubes. Get sweet, in-season blueberries for the best results.

INGREDIENTS

1 pint fresh blueberries

1 lemon, sliced, seeds removed

24 ounces filtered or distilled water

1 Chop up your fruit so that the pieces will fit into your ice cube tray, and then place the pieces in each individual mold.

2 Pour water into the tray, and carefully transfer it to the freezer. Freeze until the cubes are solid, and then use in your drink of choice.

Strawberry Grapefruit

The slight bitterness of the grapefruit is delicious when paired with sweet strawberry. These are perfect for sparkling wine or champagne.

1 Chop up your fruit so that the pieces will fit into your ice cube tray, and then place the pieces in each individual mold.

2 Pour water into the tray, and carefully transfer it to the freezer. Freeze until the cubes are solid, and then use in your drink of choice.

INGREDIENTS

1 cup strawberries, hulled and sliced

½ grapefruit, peeled, white pith removed

24 ounces filtered or distilled water

Mixed Berry

If you have an abundance of fresh berries in the summer, this is a great way to both use them up and keep them around for a while. Mash lightly for more flavor, or leave the berries intact for a stunning visual effect.

INGREDIENTS

2 cups mixed berries of your choice (such as raspberries, blackberries, or strawberries)

24 ounces filtered or distilled water

1 Chop up your fruit so that the pieces will fit into your ice cube tray, and then place the pieces in each individual mold.

2 Pour water into the tray, and carefully transfer it to the freezer. Freeze until the cubes are solid, and then use in your drink of choice.

Rosemary Orange

These herby, citrusy cubes are delightful in a cocktail made with gin, or great to jazz up iced green tea.

1 Cut each rosemary sprig into 4 pieces, small enough to fit into your ice cube molds.

2 Chop up your orange so that the pieces will fit in your ice cube tray, and put the pieces in each individual mold. Place the rosemary on top.

3 Pour water into the tray, and carefully transfer it to the freezer. Freeze until the cubes are solid, and then use in your drink of choice.

Tip: To pick a juicy orange, choose those that are heavy for their size, and have a uniform color with no green. When you smell the navel of the orange, it should smell sweet and fruity.

INGREDIENTS

6 sprigs fresh rosemary

1 orange, sliced, seeds removed

24 ounces filtered or distilled water

Cranberry Orange

Add these festive and cheery cubes to a holiday punch bowl and get everyone talking.

INGREDIENTS

24 cranberries

1 orange, peeled, seeds removed

24 ounces filtered or distilled water

1 Chop up your fruit so that the pieces will fit into your ice cube tray, and then place the pieces in each individual mold.

2 Pour water into the tray, and carefully transfer it to the freezer. Freeze until the cubes are solid, and then use in your drink of choice.

Note: Fresh cranberries are usually only found in the winter, but if you can't find fresh, frozen will work in this recipe.

Orange Vanilla Almond

These ice cubes are creamy, fragrant, and sweet. Perfect for adding to ice tea or just plain water.

1 Chop up your orange into pieces that will fit into your ice cube trays.

2 Add the water and extracts to a pitcher and stir to combine. Pour contents of pitcher into ice cube tray and place orange pieces into each individual mold. Freeze until solid.

INGREDIENTS

1 orange, peeled, seeds removed

1 teaspoon almond extract

½ teaspoon vanilla extract

24 ounces filtered or distilled water

Kiwi Melon

Kiwi and melon are a great combination; the sweet, juicy flavor is the perfect pick-me-up when you need to hydrate, but still want something tasty.

INGREDIENTS

1 kiwi, peeled

1 cup cubed cantaloupe or honeydew melon

24 ounces filtered or distilled water

1 Chop up your fruit so that the pieces will fit into your ice cube tray, and then place the pieces in each individual mold.

2 Pour water into the tray, and carefully transfer it to the freezer. Freeze until the cubes are solid, and then use in your drink of choice.

Mango Strawberry

Brightly colored mango and juicy red strawberries pair perfectly in these fragrant cubes. Make sure your mango is extra ripe for the best flavor.

1 Chop up your fruit so that the pieces will fit into your ice cube tray, and then place the pieces in each individual mold.

2 Pour water into the tray, and carefully transfer it to the freezer. Freeze until the cubes are solid, and then use in your drink of choice.

INGREDIENTS

1 mango, peeled and diced

½ cup strawberries, hulled and sliced

24 ounces filtered or distilled water

Pineapple Coconut

Pineapple and coconut is a match made in heaven, and these coconut water cubes prove that beyond a doubt! These are delicious in a cocktail made with rum, but are also good in iced green tea.

INGREDIENTS

1 cup finely chopped pineapple

24 ounces coconut water

1 Place the pineapple in your ice cube molds.

2 Pour the coconut water over the pineapple and freeze until the cubes are firm.

Raspberry Coconut

Coconut water really benefits from any fruit you add in, but raspberries are particularly tasty. These cubes mix well in rum cocktails, as well as iced teas.

1 Chop up your berries so that the pieces will fit into your ice cube tray, and then place the pieces in each individual mold.

2 Pour coconut water into the tray, and carefully transfer it to the freezer. Freeze until the cubes are solid, and then use in your drink of choice.

INGREDIENTS

1 pint raspberries, lightly muddled

24 ounces coconut water

Cherry Vanilla

MAKES 24 ICE CUBES

Dark, sweet cherries become heavenly when paired with the floral aroma of vanilla. If you drink an occasional soda, make it extra special with these cubes.

INGREDIENTS

24 fresh cherries, pitted

1 teaspoon pure vanilla extract

24 ounces filtered or distilled water

1 Chop up your cherries so that the pieces will fit in your ice cube tray, and put the pieces in each individual mold.

2 Stir the vanilla into the water and pour over the cherries.

3 Carefully transfer the tray to the freezer. Freeze until the cubes are solid, and then use in your drink of choice.

Blueberry Lemon Almond

These are simply amazing in fresh lemonade or iced tea on a hot summer day. Make these for your next backyard barbecue and wait for the rave reviews to come rolling in!

1 Chop up your fruit so that the pieces will fit into your ice cube tray, and then place the pieces in each individual mold.

2 Stir the almond extract into the water, and pour over the fruit.

3 Carefully transfer the tray to the freezer. Freeze until the cubes are solid, and then use in your drink of choice.

INGREDIENTS

1 lemon, sliced, seeds removed

1 pint blueberries

1 teaspoon pure almond extract

24 ounces filtered or distilled water

Peach Almond

If you can get your hands on tree-ripened peaches, use them for these ice cubes and you won't be disappointed. These are best in fresh-brewed iced tea.

INGREDIENTS

1 fresh, ripe peach, pitted and sliced

1 teaspoon pure almond extract

24 ounces filtered or distilled water

1 Chop up the peach so that the pieces will fit into your ice cube tray, and then place the pieces in each individual mold.

2 Stir the almond extract into the water, and pour over the fruit.

3 Carefully transfer the tray to the freezer. Freeze until the cubes are solid, and then use in your drink of choice.

Watermelon Coconut

These taste like summer in a glass, and are an amazing way to add flavor to plain old water on a hot day.

1 Chop up the watermelon so that the pieces will fit into your ice cube tray, and then place the pieces in each individual mold.

2 Pour coconut water into the tray, and carefully transfer it to the freezer. Freeze until the cubes are solid, and then use in your drink of choice.

INGREDIENTS

1 cup cubed watermelon

24 ounces coconut water

Coconut Key Lime

These cubes will take you on a tropical vacation whenever you need one. These are delicious with tequila, but can also jazz up your daily dose of H_2O. If you can't find key limes, regular limes will do.

INGREDIENTS

6 key limes, sliced or quartered

24 ounces coconut water

1 Chop up your limes so that the pieces will fit in your ice cube tray, and place the pieces in each individual mold.

2 Pour coconut water over the limes, and carefully transfer the tray to the freezer. Freeze until the cubes are solid, and then use in your drink of choice.

Strawberry Pomegranate

These sweet, tart cubes are perfect in a punch bowl full of lemonade, as the contrasting colors make a beautiful presentation.

1 Chop up your strawberries so that the pieces will fit in your ice cube tray, and place the pieces in each individual mold. Divide the pomegranate seeds evenly between the molds.

2 Pour water into the tray, and carefully transfer it to the freezer. Freeze until the cubes are solid, and then use in your drink of choice.

Tip: You can usually find pomegranate seeds in the produce section of your grocery store, which means you can skip the messy step of seeding a whole pomegranate.

INGREDIENTS

1 cup strawberries, hulled and chopped

½ cup pomegranate seeds

24 ounces filtered or distilled water

Maraschino Cherry

The kids at your party will appreciate these cubes in their Shirley Temples, but they're pretty good in adult drinks as well, especially those made with bourbon.

INGREDIENTS

24 cherries

24 ounces filtered or distilled water

1 Put a cherry in each individual ice mold, and pour the water over top.

2 Freeze until the cubes are solid, and then use in your drink of choice.

Tip: For an extra stunning visual effect, leave the stems on the cherries so that they stick out of the top of the cube. And remember: double-boil your water so that your ice is clear as day!

Vegetables

Vegetables can be made into ice cubes just as easily as fruit. The results will be earthier and less sweet, but still delicious and refreshing.

Don't hesitate to use these in cocktails. You can also add them to water when you need extra hydration and nutrients.

Cucumber Mint

Looking for a refreshing, skin-clearing chiller? These ice cubes are the solution you've been searching for. Remember to remove all the seeds from your cucumber before making your ice cubes.

1 Chop up your cucumber so that the pieces will fit into your ice cube tray, and place the pieces in each individual mold. Top each with a mint leaf.

2 Pour water into the tray, and carefully transfer it to the freezer. Freeze until the cubes are solid, and then use in your drink of choice.

INGREDIENTS

1 cucumber, sliced and seeded

24 small mint leaves, lightly muddled

24 ounces filtered or distilled water

Tomato Basil

MAKES 24 ICE CUBES

This classic combination is good for more than just sauce. Add these to a Bloody Mary, or use them to boost plain-old tomato juice.

INGREDIENTS

24 cherry tomatoes, halved

24 small basil leaves, lightly muddled

24 ounces filtered or distilled water

1 Chop up your tomatoes so that the pieces will fit in your ice cube tray, and place the pieces in each individual mold. Top each mold with a basil leaf.

2 Pour water into the tray, and carefully transfer it to the freezer. Freeze until the cubes are solid, and then use in your drink of choice.

Tip: If you're making these for a party or event, use multicolored tomatoes for a stunning visual effect!

Lemon Fennel

These are a favorite of mine for iced tea, as the anise-flavored fennel adds a new dimension to the tart lemon and bitter tea.

1 Chop up your lemon and fennel so that the pieces will fit in your ice cube tray, and place the pieces in each individual mold.

2 Pour water into the tray, and carefully transfer it to the freezer. Freeze until the cubes are solid, and then use in your drink of choice.

INGREDIENTS

1 lemon, sliced, seeds removed

1 cup chopped fennel

24 ounces filtered or distilled water

Melon Radish

These spicy ice cubes add vigor to plain water. It sounds like an odd combination, but the sweetness of the melon plays nicely off the pungent radishes.

INGREDIENTS

1 cup cubed honeydew melon or cantaloupe

2 radishes, scrubbed and thinly sliced

24 ounces filtered or distilled water

1 Chop up your produce so that the pieces will fit into your ice cube tray, and then place the pieces in each individual mold.

2 Pour water into the tray, and carefully transfer it to the freezer. Freeze until the cubes are solid, and then use in your drink of choice.

Cilantro Jalapeño

These spicy herb cubes are absolutely amazing in pineapple juice — the heat plays nicely against the sweet flavor of the pineapple. If you can make your own fresh-squeezed juice, it's even better.

1 Place the peppers in an ice cube tray and top with the cilantro leaves.

2 Pour water into the tray, and carefully transfer it to the freezer. Freeze until the cubes are solid, and then use in your drink of choice.

INGREDIENTS

2 jalapeño peppers, sliced, seeds removed

24 cilantro leaves

24 ounces filtered or distilled water

Herbs and Spices

These cubes are mostly made of fruit, but with the added dimensions of herbs and spices. Woody herbs and whole spices add a cozy, warm flavor to your ice, and do a great job to compliment the brightness that comes from the fruit.

Cinnamon Coffee

These cubes are delicious in your morning iced coffee, making your morning trip to the local coffee shop almost unnecessary. They're a great way to use up leftover coffee from your pot instead of pouring it down the drain.

INGREDIENTS

1 teaspoon cinnamon

24 ounces fresh-brewed coffee, cooled

1 Stir the cinnamon into the coffee, and pour into ice cube molds.

2 Transfer the tray to freezer and freeze until the cubes are solid.

Watermelon Thyme

MAKES 24 ICE CUBES

Earthy and sweet, these cubes are delicious in lemonade, and if you feel like imbibing, try them in a gin-based cocktail.

1 Chop up your watermelon so that the pieces will fit in your ice cube tray, and place the pieces in each individual mold. Sprinkle the thyme over each mold.

2 Pour water into the tray, and carefully transfer it to the freezer. Freeze until the cubes are solid, and then use in your drink of choice.

INGREDIENTS

1 cup cubed watermelon

1 tablespoon fresh thyme leaves

24 ounces filtered or distilled water

Cilantro Lime

For an extra special margarita, you can't go wrong with these cubes. They're also delicious in cold ginger ale.

INGREDIENTS

1 lime, sliced

24 cilantro leaves

24 ounces filtered or distilled water

1 Chop up your lime so that the pieces will fit into your ice cube tray, and then place the pieces in each individual mold. Top with the cilantro.

2 Pour water into the tray, and carefully transfer it to the freezer. Freeze until the cubes are solid, and then use in your drink of choice.

Ginger Green Tea

You don't have to make ice cubes out of just water, as these delicately flavored tea cubes will show.

1 Stir the ginger into the tea. Pour into ice cube molds and transfer to the freezer.

2 Freeze until the cubes are solid.

Nutrition Note: Green tea is loaded with antioxidants, and can aid in weight loss. Ginger is a natural remedy for an upset stomach, making these powerful cubes a healing component in any drink or smoothie.

INGREDIENTS

24 ounces fresh-brewed green tea, cooled

1 tablespoon grated ginger

Apple Cinnamon

MAKES 24 ICE CUBES

Put these in a whiskey-based cocktail, or enjoy them in the fall if you like cold apple cider. Sweet and spicy, they hit the spot on an early autumn evening.

INGREDIENTS

1 apple, cored and thinly sliced

1 teaspoon cinnamon

24 ounces filtered or distilled water

1 Chop up your apple so that the pieces will fit into your ice cube tray, and then place the pieces in each individual mold. Sprinkle the cinnamon over each mold.

2 Pour water into the tray, and carefully transfer it to the freezer. Freeze until the cubes are solid, and then use in your drink of choice.

Lavender Sage

For an upscale lemonade, these fragrant cubes can't be beat. They're perfect for a bridal shower, in a big punch bowl.

1 Sprinkle the lavender into your ice cube tray, and top each mold with a sage leaf.

2 Pour water into the tray, and carefully transfer it to the freezer. Freeze until the cubes are solid, and then use in your drink of choice.

INGREDIENTS

1 teaspoon culinary lavender

24 small sage leaves

24 ounces filtered or distilled water

Black Tea Grapefruit

Rich tannins from the tea are perfect when infused with grapefruit. Add these to your pitcher of iced tea in the summer, and it will never be watered down!

INGREDIENTS

24 ounces fresh-brewed black tea, cooled

1 grapefruit, peeled, white pith removed

1 Chop up your grapefruit so that the pieces will fit into your ice cube tray, and then place the pieces in each individual mold.

2 Pour the tea into the tray, and carefully transfer it to the freezer. Freeze until the cubes are solid, and then use in your drink of choice.

Cherry Basil

You can use sweet or tart cherries in these refreshing cubes. The pretty color makes them perfect for backyard barbecues and pitchers of fresh-squeezed lemonade.

1 Chop up your cherries so that the pieces will fit into your ice cube tray, and then place the pieces in each individual mold. Top each with a basil leaf.

2 Pour water into the tray, and carefully transfer it to the freezer. Freeze until the cubes are solid, and then use in your drink of choice.

INGREDIENTS

24 pitted fresh cherries

24 small basil leaves, lightly muddled

24 ounces filtered or distilled water

Mixed Herb

A combination of herbs makes these cubes perfect for when you want to add a vegetal note to your drink. Use in iced tea, lemonade, or even lemon-lime soda.

INGREDIENTS

2 tablespoons fresh thyme leaves

2 tablespoons fresh chopped parsley

2 tablespoons fresh chopped mint

24 ounces filtered or distilled water

1 Divide the chopped herbs between the molds in your ice cube tray.

2 Pour water into the tray, and carefully transfer it to the freezer. Freeze until the cubes are solid, and then use in your drink of choice.

Substitution Suggestion: You can use whatever herbs you have or like, so don't limit yourself to those listed here. Rosemary and thyme is a good combination, as is basil and mint.

Mango Pineapple Mint

Add these to a cold glass of coconut water for a hydrating treat. Be sure to not overdo it when you're muddling the mint—it can make your ice bitter!

1 Chop up your fruit so that the pieces will fit into your ice cube tray, and then place the pieces in each individual mold. Top with mint leaves.

2 Pour water into the tray, and carefully transfer it to the freezer. Freeze until the cubes are solid, and then use in your drink of choice.

INGREDIENTS

½ cup finely diced mango

½ cup finely diced pineapple

24 small, fresh mint leaves, lightly muddled

24 ounces filtered or distilled water

Strawberry Peppercorn

MAKES 24 ICE CUBES

This unique combination is exotic and fruity. The peppercorns lend a hint of spice to the fragrant berry notes, which is outstanding in plain old water.

INGREDIENTS

1 cup strawberries, hulled and chopped

1 teaspoon fresh ground black pepper

24 ounces filtered or distilled water

1 Place the berries in the ice cube molds and sprinkle pepper over them.

2 Pour water into the tray, and carefully transfer it to the freezer. Freeze until the cubes are solid, and then use in your drink of choice.

Tip: Use whole peppercorns and either grind them or smash them with a mortar and pestle. Don't use powdered black pepper—it's got fillers and preservatives that won't impart the clean flavor you're looking for.

Cinnamon Honey Almond Milk

MAKES 24 ICE CUBES

These creamy, slightly spicy cubes are a great way to jazz up your morning smoothie. Make sure to use unsweetened almond milk, as you want the sweetness to come from the honey.

1 Stir the honey and cinnamon into the almond milk until they are thoroughly combined.

2 Pour into ice cube molds and freeze until the cubes are solid.

INGREDIENTS

2 tablespoons honey

½ teaspoon ground cinnamon

24 ounces unsweetened almond milk

Ginger Rosemary Lemongrass

MAKES 24 ICE CUBES

Earthy and spicy with a hint of citrus, these cubes will take your summer lemonade to a whole new level! Due to the ginger in the water, these ice cubes will be cloudy regardless of boiling, so you can skip that step.

INGREDIENTS

6 sprigs fresh rosemary

2 stalks lemongrass

1 tablespoon grated ginger

24 ounces filtered or distilled water

1 Cut each rosemary sprig into 4 pieces, small enough to fit into your ice cube molds. Slice the lemongrass into 24 pieces and put one in each mold.

2 Stir the grated ginger into your water, and carefully pour over the lemongrass and rosemary.

3 Carefully transfer the tray to the freezer. Freeze until the cubes are solid, and then use in your drink of choice.

Lemon Basil

Lemon and basil are a classic combination for a reason, and these ice cubes are no exception. Throw a few of these in your water bottle before you leave for the day, and you'll have no trouble remaining hydrated all day long.

1 Chop up your lemon so that the pieces will fit into your ice cube tray, and then place the pieces in each individual mold. Add a basil leaf to each mold.

2 Pour water into the tray, and carefully transfer it to the freezer. Freeze until the cubes are solid, and then use in your drink of choice.

INGREDIENTS

1 lemon, sliced, seeds removed

24 small basil leaves, lightly muddled

24 ounces filtered or distilled water

Flowers

Flowers are perfect for ice cubes because they are so pretty and colorful. They add subtle flavor to ice, but even more than that, they add an amazing amount of beauty.

For this reason, I would make sure to boil your water twice before making these, so that the colors come through loud and clear.

Vanilla Rose Petal

These flowery, fragrant cubes are amazing in iced green tea. Perfect for when you want something subtle, but not boring!

INGREDIENTS

1 teaspoon vanilla extract

24 food-grade rose petals

24 ounces filtered or distilled water

1 Place the rose petals in your ice cube tray.

2 Combine the water and vanilla extract, and pour over the rose petals. Freeze until the cubes are solid, and then use in your drink of choice.

Lavender Lemon Vanilla

Lavender and lemon is a heavenly combination, but when you add vanilla, it takes it up a notch. You'll barely be able to believe it.

1 Chop up your lemon so that the pieces will fit into your ice cube tray, and then place the pieces in each individual mold. Add the lavender to each mold.

2 Add the vanilla to the water, pour the water into the tray, and carefully transfer the tray to the freezer. Freeze until the cubes are solid, and then use in your drink of choice.

INGREDIENTS

1 lemon, sliced, seeds removed

½ teaspoon culinary lavender

1 teaspoon pure vanilla extract

24 ounces filtered
or distilled water

Blueberry Lavender

Make some fresh-squeezed lemonade sweetened with honey, and then add these blended cubes for a refreshing, tasty summer beverage that quite simply can't be beat!

INGREDIENTS

1 cup fresh blueberries

½ teaspoon culinary lavender

24 ounces filtered water

1 Place the blueberries into your ice cube tray and sprinkle the lavender evenly over them.

2 Pour water into the tray and carefully transfer to the freezer. Freeze until the cubes are solid, and then use in your favorite drink.

Lemon Chamomile

These subtly flavored cubes are a great addition to your water bottle when you know you'll have a stressful day. Just breathe in the scent for a minute before sipping, and you're on the way to instant relaxation.

1 Chop up the lemon and flowers so that the pieces will fit in your ice cube tray, and place the pieces in each individual mold.

2 Pour water into the tray, and carefully transfer it to the freezer. Freeze until the cubes are solid, and then use in your drink of choice.

INGREDIENTS

1 lemon, sliced, seeds removed

24 chamomile flowers, fresh or dried

24 ounces filtered or distilled water

Violet

Violets have spicy notes of vanilla, making these single-ingredient cubes perfect for iced tea. Or add them to a big jug of water for a pretty indulgence. You can use candied violets to add a bit of sweetness to your drink as the cubes melt.

INGREDIENTS

24 food-safe violets

24 ounces filtered or distilled water

1 Add the flowers to your ice cube tray, chopping if necessary.

2 Pour water into the tray, and carefully transfer it to the freezer. Freeze until the cubes are solid, and then use in your drink of choice.

Mocktails

Having a party can be tricky when you know some of your guests don't drink. You can always have iced tea or soda on hand, of course, but if you have a signature cocktail, you may want non-drinkers to feel more welcome.

The answer to this dilemma is easy: Mocktails! These fruity, sweet drinks are an easy way to make everyone feel welcome. In this chapter, you'll find a variety of delicious non-alcoholic drinks that you can serve at parties or just keep in the fridge.

Some of these recipes use the infused water in this book, so read through the recipes to see what you'll need to do beforehand to get them ready.

Simple Syrup

MAKES ABOUT 1 CUP

Many of the recipes in this section are sweetened with simple syrup, an easy, homemade syrup made with sugar and water, and then infused with a flavor. Simple syrup is preferred over granulated sugar because you won't end up with sugar crystals in your drink. Here is an easy recipe for simple syrup that will work in all of the mocktails in this book, as well as any of your favorite cold beverages:

INGREDIENTS

1 cup water

1 cup granulated sugar

Flavor enhancers of your choice: 2-3 fresh herb sprigs, fresh flowers, vanilla bean, cinnamon stick, etc.

1 Place the water and sugar in a medium saucepan and bring to a simmer over medium heat. Simmer for about 5 minutes, until all of the sugar is dissolved. Remove from heat, let cool, and transfer to an airtight container.

2 To infuse your syrup, add your flavoring agent to the cooled syrup and allow to infuse for about an hour. Remove the agent before the using.

Tip: Once you have made the syrup, it can be stored in the refrigerator for about a week.

Sparkling Grapefruit and Rosemary

You can use store-bought grapefruit juice for these, but if you have a juicer, this is the time to use it. Serve these in pretty glasses and garnish each with a rosemary sprig.

1 Combine the grapefruit juice and sparkling water in a pitcher filled with ice. Add the rosemary syrup.

2 Serve over ice, if preferred, and garnish each glass with a small sprig of rosemary.

Tip: Instead of plain seltzer, you can use the Citrus Rosemary water (see page 121) made with sparkling, rather than still.

INGREDIENTS

16 ounces grapefruit juice

16 ounces sparkling water

Simple syrup infused with rosemary, to taste

Rosemary sprigs, for garnish

Basil Peach Lemonade

This is perfect for a summer barbecue, especially if you can get fresh peaches and basil from your local farmers' market. Garnish with peach slices and basil leaves.

INGREDIENTS

16 ounces filtered water

1 small bunch basil, stems removed

4 ripe peaches, peeled and pitted

1 cup lemon juice (about 6 lemons)

Simple syrup infused with basil, to taste

1 Place the peaches in a blender or food processor and puree until smooth, adding a tablespoon or two of water to help them along, if necessary.

2 Strain the peach puree through a fine mesh strainer and transfer the mixture to a pitcher.

3 Add the lemon juice, filtered water, and simple syrup.

4 Serve over ice and garnish with fresh basil leaves, lemon, or peach slices.

Serving Idea: Skewer basil leaves, cubed peaches, and tiny lemon wedges on toothpicks or cocktail stirrers for a cute, fun garnish.

Cherry Limeade

This mocktail is fun and festive, and perfect for adults and kids alike! It's especially fun when served with the Maraschino Cherry ice cubes (see page 164).

INGREDIENTS

1 Combine the spritzer, lime juice, cherries and their juices in a large pitcher. Add simple syrup.

2 Serve over ice, and garnish with lime slices.

Tip: While bottled lime juice seems like an easier option, you'll get a much better flavor using fresh-squeezed lime juice. A citrus juicer is an inexpensive tool that is easy to use and will help you get the most out of your citrus.

64 ounces Cherry-Lime Spritzer (see page 30)

1 cup lime juice (about 4-5 limes)

1 10-ounce jar of maraschino cherries, including juice

Simple syrup, to taste

Lime slices, for garnish

Maraschino Cherry ice cubes, optional

Blood Orange Strawberry Soda

This bright red, sweet, tart, homemade soda is a hit no matter where you serve it. If you can't find blood oranges, regular oranges will do.

INGREDIENTS

1 cup fresh strawberries, hulled

1 cup fresh-squeezed blood orange juice (about 4 blood oranges)

48 ounces sparkling water

Simple syrup, to taste

1 Place the strawberries in a blender or food processor with 2 tablespoons water and puree until smooth. Strain through a fine mesh strainer into a pitcher.

2 Add the orange juice and sparkling water, and stir. Sweeten to taste with the simple syrup.

3 Serve over ice.

Serving Idea: Make candied blood orange slices by adding thinly sliced blood oranges to your simple syrup. Simmer for about 10 minutes, carefully remove the slices, and let dry on a parchment-lined baking sheet. Cut in half and use to carefully garnish the serving glasses. You can also use the simple syrup to sweeten your mocktail. You can also serve these with the Strawberry Grapefruit ice cubes (page 135) for an extra special treat.

Chai Cider

This fragrant and spicy apple cider can be served hot or cold, so it's perfect on those fall days where you still want a taste of autumn, but the summer hasn't quite gone away.

1 Put all of the ingredients in a medium saucepan and bring to a boil. Reduce to a low simmer and continue cooking for 15-20 minutes.

2 Turn off heat and strain into a pitcher. Serve hot, or let cool and serve over ice.

INGREDIENTS

4 cups apple cider

1 piece ginger about an inch, peeled

2 cinnamon sticks

4 whole cloves

4 cardamom pods, smashed

4 whole peppercorns

1 star anise

Sparkling Mango Mocktail

MAKES 6 SERVINGS

Ripened mango is fragrant, dreamy, and sweet. When combined with sparkling water, it's indulgent and fun. This mocktail is delicious poured over the Coconut Key Lime ice cubes (see page 160) from this book, so if you're serving this at a party, it's worth the extra step to make those in advance.

INGREDIENTS

2 ripened mangos, peeled, pits removed

48 ounces sparkling water

Simple syrup, to taste

Coconut Key Lime ice cubes, optional

1 Place the mango pieces in a blender with 2 tablespoons water and blend until smooth. Strain the mixture through a fine mesh sieve into a pitcher.

2 Add the sparkling water, and then stir in simple syrup.

3 Serve over ice.

Classic Shirley Temple

While usually served to kids at adult parties, there's no reason adults can't enjoy this fruity drink as well.

1 Combine the Grenadine and Citrus Fizz. Add the simple syrup.

2 Serve over ice.

Serving Suggestion: For a party, serve this with a combination of Maraschino Cherry ice cubes (see page 164) and the Simple Citrus Cubes (see page 128). Float them in the punch bowl and watch everyone gravitate toward this famed kiddie cocktail.

INGREDIENTS

12 ounces Grenadine

64 ounces Citrus Fizz (see page 25)

Simple syrup, to taste

Maraschino Cherry ice cubes, optional

Simple Citrus ice cubes, optional

Cucumber Mint Lemonade

Cucumber and mint are both perfect for infusions, because the flavor comes fast with no extra work. That makes this the perfect last-minute beverage for a backyard barbecue or birthday party.

INGREDIENTS

32 ounces filtered water

1 small cucumber, sliced, seeds removed

1 bunch mint leaves

2 cups lemon juice (about 12 lemons)

Simple syrup, to taste

1 Place all of the ingredients in a pitcher with ice. Sweeten with the simple syrup.

2 Chill until ready to serve.

Citrus Cranberry Punch

This is a classic punch recipe that is great for birthday parties, showers, or any special occasion. Float orange slices and Cranberry Orange ice cubes (see page 140) in your bowl or pitcher for an extra touch.

1 Combine the cranberry juice, water, and orange juice in a pitcher or punch bowl. Add simple syrup, to taste.

2 Serve over ice.

INGREDIENTS

32 ounces cranberry juice

32 ounces Citrus Fizz (see page 25)

1 cup orange juice

Simple syrup, to taste

Cranberry Orange ice cubes, optional

Tropical Berry Punch

This fruity and refreshing punch has a beautiful bright color, and a sweetness both adults and kids will love. Mixed Berry ice cubes (see page 136) are the perfect accompaniment, and look especially good when floating next to orange slices, or a skewer of fruit.

INGREDIENTS

32 ounces Mixed Berry water (see page 38) made with seltzer

32 ounces Tropical Spritzer water (see page 53) made with seltzer

1 cup cranberry juice

1 cup orange juice

Simple syrup, to taste

Mixed Berry ice cubes, optional

Orange slices, optional

1 Combine the waters, cranberry juice, and orange juice in a pitcher or punch bowl. Add simple syrup.

2 Serve over ice.

Ginger Lime Spritzer

This light and refreshing mocktail is great for brunches, showers, or anywhere else you want something that's not overpowering.

1 Combine the ginger ale, water, and lime juice in a pitcher and stir. Add simple syrup.

2 Serve over ice.

INGREDIENTS

32 ounces ginger ale

32 ounces Orange Ginger Spritzer (see page 32)

1 cup lime juice

Simple syrup, to taste

Sparkling Watermelon Limeade

MAKES 8 SERVINGS

This refreshing, bright-pink drink says summer like nothing else. It's best made with in-season watermelon and fresh lime juice, and is lovely when garnished with a lime wedge.

INGREDIENTS

1 cup watermelon cubes, seeds removed

32 ounces sparkling water

1 cup lime juice

Simple syrup, to taste

1 Place the watermelon in a blender or food processor and puree until smooth, adding a tablespoon or two of water if necessary. Strain through a fine mesh sieve.

2 Combine the watermelon puree, sparkling water, and lime juice with the simple syrup.

3 Serve chilled, with lime or watermelon wedges for garnish.

Serving Idea: To impress guests at a party, salt the rim of your serving glasses, as you would for margaritas. Salt brings out the sweetness of watermelon, and the salted rims add a nice touch that is otherwise forgotten for non-alcoholic drinks.

Vanilla Berry Spritzer

Berries pureed with vanilla combine with sparkling water to make an interesting, delicious, non-alcoholic beverage that everyone will enjoy. Use fresh summer berries to ensure bright, juicy flavor.

INGREDIENTS

½ cup sliced strawberries

½ cup blackberries

½ cup raspberries

1 teaspoon vanilla extract

64 ounces sparkling water

Simple syrup, to taste

1 Place the berries and vanilla in a blender or food processor with 2-3 tablespoons water. Puree until smooth and then strain through a fine mesh sieve.

2 Combine the berry puree and sparkling water in a pitcher. Then add the simple syrup.

3 Serve over ice, with additional fresh berries as a garnish.

Serving Idea: Pour this over the Mixed Berry ice cubes (page 136) for even more berry flavor.

Lavender Coconut Lemonade

This unique lemonade uses fragrant lavender and coconut water, which pair beautifully with the tart lemons. Perfect for an outdoor brunch on a sunny day when you want to guarantee a relaxing time.

INGREDIENTS

32 ounces coconut water

2 cups lemon juice (about 12 lemons)

Simple syrup infused with 2 lavender flowers, to taste

Lavender flowers and lemon slices, for garnish

Lavender Lemon Vanilla ice cubes (see page 219), optional

1 Combine the coconut water and lemon juice. Add the lavender-infused syrup.

2 Serve over ice, and garnish with lavender flowers and lemon slices.

Serving Idea: Paper straws come in all different colors and are perfect for serving drinks like this. Pick up the striped variety in both purple and yellow to add a festive touch to your drinks.

Herbed Pineapple Lemonade

This refreshingly flavored lemonade is sweet and tart, with a green hue thanks to the herb-infused syrup. You can use any herb you want here, but more than two may overwhelm your drink. My suggestions are basil and either mint or cilantro, but you can use any of your favorites.

1 Combine the water, pineapple juice, and lemon juice in a pitcher. Add simple syrup.

2 Serve over ice.

INGREDIENTS

32 ounces filtered water

32 ounces pineapple juice

1 cup lemon juice (from about 6 lemons)

Herb-infused simple syrup, to taste

Index

ABOUT THE AUTHOR

Amy Hunter is a culinary arts graduate, and has been writing about and photographing food for the past 10 years. She has ghostwritten numerous cookbooks, written blog posts for various brands and companies, and has spent hundreds of hours testing recipes with products like avocado oil and sea salt.

When she is not cooking in her kitchen, she is traveling the world, seeing a Broadway musical, or spending time with her husband and her dog.

You can find more about her and her work at www.tinyredkitchen.com.

ABOUT CIDER MILL PRESS BOOK PUBLISHERS

Good ideas ripen with time. From seed to harvest, Cider Mill
Press brings fine reading, information, and entertainment
together between the covers of its creatively crafted books.
Our Cider Mill bears fruit twice a year, publishing
a new crop of titles each spring and fall.

"Where Good Books Are Ready for Press"

VISIT US ON THE WEB AT
www.cidermillpress.com

OR WRITE TO US AT
12 Spring Street
PO Box 454
Kennebunkport, Maine 04046